Dinosaurs Discovered

by Dean R. Lomax

Editors Katy Lennon, Kritika Gupta, Abhijit Dutta
Project Art Editors Emma Hobson, Yamini Panwar
Art Editor Shubham Rohatgi
US Editor Jennette ElNaggar
US Senior Editor Shannon Beatty
Jacket Coordinator Francesca Young
Jacket Designer Dheeraj Arora
DTP Designers Dheeraj Singh, Mohd Rizwan
Picture Researcher Sakshi Saluja
Producer, Pre-Production Dragana Puvacic
Producer Barbara Ossàwska
Managing Editors Laura Gilbert, Monica Saigal
Managing Art Editor Diane Peyton Jones
Deputy Managing Art Editor Ivy Sengupta
Delhi Team Head Malavika Talukder
Creative Director Helen Senior
Publishing Director Sarah Larter

Reading Consultant Linda Gambrell
Educational Consultant Jacqueline Harris

First American Edition, 2018
Published in the United States by DK Publishing
345 Hudson Street, New York, New York 10014

Copyright © 2018 Dorling Kindersley Limited
DK, a Division of Penguin Random House LLC
18 19 20 21 22 10 9 8 7 6 5 4 3 2 1
001–310460–Oct/18

A catalog record for this book is available from the Library of Congress.
ISBN: 978-1-4654-7729-3 (Paperback)
ISBN: 978-1-4654-7730-9 (Hardcover)

DK books are available at special discounts when purchased in bulk for sales promotions,
premiums, fund-raising, or educational use. For details, contact:
DK Publishing Special Markets,
345 Hudson Street, New York, New York 10014
SpecialSales@dk.com

Printed and bound in China.

A WORLD OF IDEAS:
SEE ALL THERE IS TO KNOW

www.dk.com

Contents

Styracosaurus. The dinosaur illustrations shown in this book are artists' ideas of how dinosaurs might have looked, based on the scientific evidence available.

Chapter 1

Who Studies Dinosaurs?

From vast deserts to high mountains, dinosaur bones are found all around the world. Each new dinosaur discovery has its own story to tell about prehistoric life.

A team of paleontologists, including Dean Lomax (left), at an excavation site.

People who study dinosaurs and prehistoric life are called paleontologists. They are interested in everything from dinosaurs to plants to mammoths and fossilized poops—called coprolites! Fossils are the remains, or traces, of prehistoric animals and plants that have been left in rocks. They can be preserved in rocks for millions of years and can give us clues about the history of our planet.

From fossils, paleontologists can find out what dinosaurs ate, how big they were, and even what color they were. People of all ages find dinosaurs interesting, and right now, there are more paleontologists than there have ever been before.

A coprolite made by a prehistoric shark.

Only a tiny number of animals are ever found as fossils. For a dinosaur to become a fossil, it must have died in special conditions. Many fossils are created when an animal dies close to (or in) water. It then becomes buried by mud or sand at the bottom of the water, called sediment. Over time, the soft parts of its body rot away, leaving just the hard parts, such as bones and teeth.

About 150 million years ago

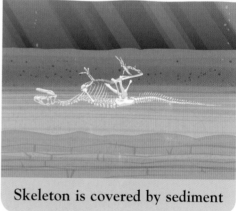

Skeleton is covered by sediment

An *Allosaurus* dies
near a river.

Over millions of years the
sediment turns to rock.

As the skeleton is buried deeper, the bones and teeth are replaced by minerals. These minerals then become the fossil. In rare examples, even the animal's skin can be found as part of the fossil.

Fossilized dinosaur skin.

Millions of years later

As rock layers form, the fossilized skeleton is buried deeper underground.

Today

The fossilized skeleton is exposed at the surface.

When paleontologists discover a new dinosaur, they get to name it. On average, paleontologists announce a new species of dinosaur every two weeks! Amazingly, more than 1,400 species are currently known.

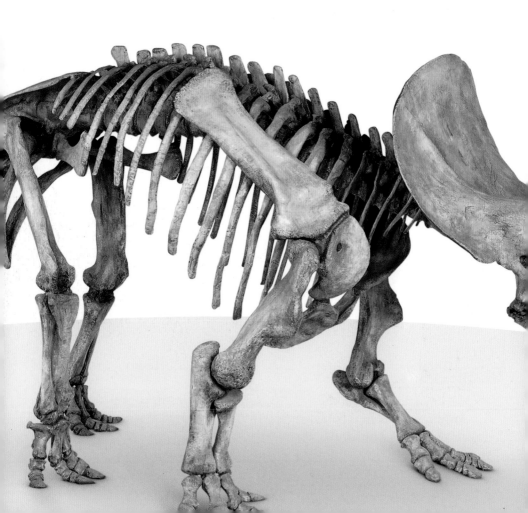

Dinosaur names are taken from Greek or Latin words. They are often named for a feature, such as sharp teeth or horns. Some dinosaurs are given names that describe how they might have behaved. Others are named after the place they were discovered or the person who found them. The word "dinosaur" means "terrible lizard."

Triceratops means three-horned face, in reference to the three horns on its skull.

Dinosaur Discoveries

Here are some of the most important events in the study of dinosaurs.

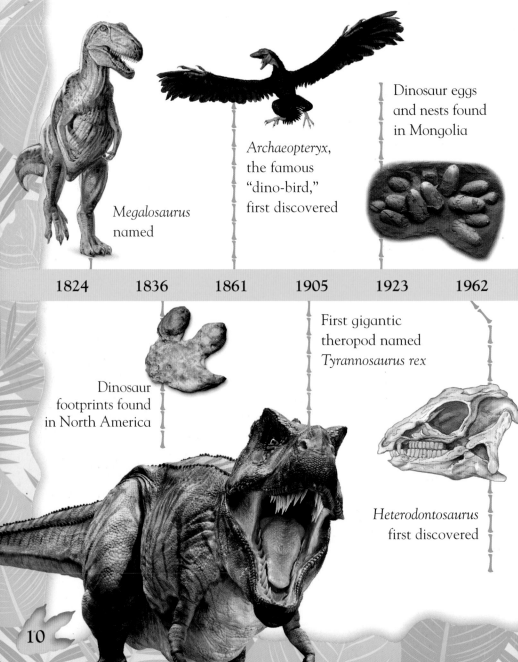

Archaeopteryx, the famous "dino-bird," first discovered

Dinosaur eggs and nests found in Mongolia

Megalosaurus named

| 1824 | 1836 | 1861 | 1905 | 1923 | 1962 |

Dinosaur footprints found in North America

First gigantic theropod named *Tyrannosaurus rex*

Heterodontosaurus first discovered

The gigantic *Argentinosaurus* is named; it is the largest dinosaur discovered so far

Scientists suggest that a comet or asteroid struck the Earth about 66 million years ago, wiping out the nonbird dinosaurs

One of the world's richest dinosaur graveyards is found in Canada

| 1979 | 1980 | 1990 | 1993 | 1997 | 2016 |

The world's most complete *T. rex* is discovered and nicknamed "Sue"

An important study shows that dinosaurs cared for their young

Part of a dinosaur tail with feathers is found in amber

Dinosaur Map

Dinosaurs lived all over the globe. Here is a map to show where some of them came from.

USA

NORTH AMERICA

UK

Tyrannosaurus

Eoraptor

SOUTH AMERICA

Argentina

Giganotosaurus

Velociraptor

Megalosaurus

EUROPE

Mongolia

Spinosaurus

ASIA

China

Egypt

AFRICA

Microraptor

Tanzania

OCEANIA

Giraffatitan

Leaellynasaura

Australia

Cryolophosaurus

ANTARCTICA

13

Chapter 2

Wonders of Europe

Many early dinosaur discoveries were made in Europe. One of the most important was the "dino-bird," *Archaeopteryx*, which was found in Germany

Archaeopteryx

in 1861. *Archaeopteryx* had a long, bony tail, sharp teeth, and feathers. It was one of the first fossils to show a close link between birds and dinosaurs. Today, paleontologists place birds and dinosaurs together in the same family.

Nearby, deep inside a Belgian coal mine in 1878, another incredible discovery was made. A herd of more than 30 *Iguanodon* skeletons were found together. It is thought that they all fell down a ravine and drowned when it flooded.

In Portugal many years later, paleontologists found fossilized dinosaur eggs. The eggs even had unborn babies preserved inside them.

An *Iguanodon* skeleton at the
Dinosaur Isle Museum, Isle of Wight, UK.

In January 1983, fossil collector William Walker was looking for fossils in a quarry in England. He found an unusual rock, which contained a large claw.

Baryonyx's claw

The Natural History Museum in London was very interested in this discovery. It sent a team to excavate, or dig, at the quarry.

The team found more than 70 percent of the dinosaur's skeleton, including a large skull with teeth in it. It was said to be the find of the century.

The dinosaur was named *Baryonyx walkeri* in William's honor. It lived about 125 million years ago, but amazingly its last meal was still preserved in its stomach. Paleontologists found that it had eaten a tasty meal of fish and other dinosaurs.

A *Baryonyx* fishing at a lake.

The largest dinosaurs to ever walk the Earth were called sauropods. They include the long-necked *Brontosaurus*.

One sauropod, named *Europasaurus*, lived about 154 million years ago. Its home was an island off the coast of Germany. The first bones were found in the mid-1990s and were closely studied by scientists. The bones showed that the adult *Europasaurus* were actually smaller than an adult African elephant.

These unusual sauropod dinosaurs were a dwarf species. Their bodies didn't grow as large as those of other sauropods because there wasn't much food for them to eat on their small island!

A roaming *Europasaurus*.

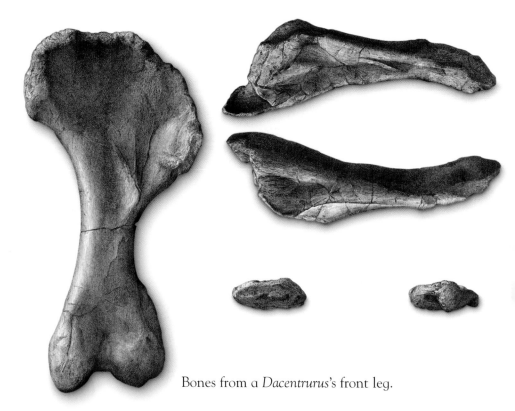

Bones from a *Dacentrurus*'s front leg.

The very first stegosaur skeleton to be discovered was found in a brick pit in Swindon, England. Stegosaurs were a group of large dinosaurs that had bony plates along their backs. They also had spikes on their tails. Workers dug up the bones in 1874 and gave them to paleontologist William Davies. He realized the bones were very important.

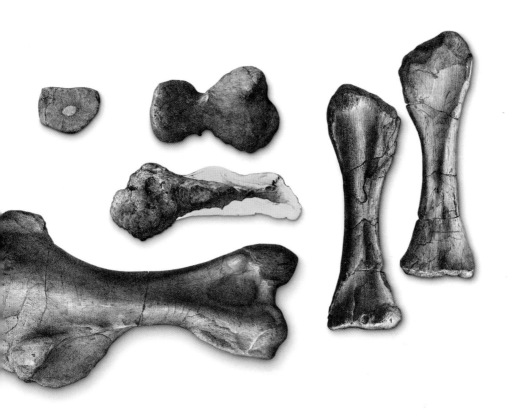

The skeleton that they found included leg bones, armor plates, and tail spines. Scientists were so excited by the discovery that many people wanted to see it. Famous paleontologist Sir Richard Owen identified the creature as a new dinosaur. It was named *Dacentrurus*, which means "very pointy tail."

Mother of Paleontology

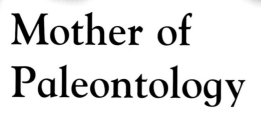

Mary Anning was a Victorian paleontologist. She lived in Lyme Regis, England, between 1799 and 1847. From a young age, she collected fossils. Here are some of her incredible discoveries.

Mary Anning's dog Tray helped her search for fossils.

Discoveries:

In 1811, Mary and her brother Joseph found a skull and skeleton in a cliff. This became the first ichthyosaur known to science. Mary was only about 12 years old.

Mary's second major discovery was the first complete plesiosaur skeleton, which she found in 1823.

In 1828, Mary found the first British pterosaur. It was later named *Dimorphodon macronyx*.

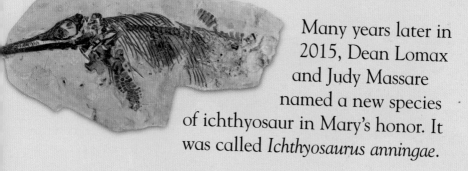

Many years later in 2015, Dean Lomax and Judy Massare named a new species of ichthyosaur in Mary's honor. It was called *Ichthyosaurus anningae*.

Dinosaur Attack

Some dinosaurs were carnivores and ate only meat. Others were herbivores and enjoyed munching on plants. Here are some of the special features that helped them to find food and survive.

Prey
This was a heavily armored herbivore. Its armor helped protect it from predators.

Sharp spikes

Ankylosaurus

Body armor

Great sense
of smell

Tyrannosaurus

Predator

This carnivore used its size,
strength, and powerful bite to
catch and eat other dinosaurs.

Clubbed tail

Powerful bite

Strong claws

25

Chapter 3

Digging in Asia

Since the 1990s, new finds in Asia have caused a lot of excitement among paleontologists. One of these was a small dinosaur from Liaoning, China, called *Sinosauropteryx*. It was named in 1996 and was the first nonbird dinosaur found with feathers.

Sinosauropteryx was about the size of a modern turkey.

One *Sinosauropteryx* was particularly well preserved. Scientists could even tell what color it was. It was reddish brown and had camouflage patterns and stripes.

Another truly remarkable dinosaur discovery was made in the Gobi Desert, Mongolia. In 1971, a fossil of a *Velociraptor* and a *Protoceratops* fighting was unearthed by a team of paleontologists. The battle had become frozen in time as the pair were buried by sand, possibly from the collapse of a sand dune.

Protoceratops

In 2002, paleontologists from China and the USA led an expedition to the desertlike area of the Junggar Basin in China. They found two small tyrannosaur skeletons, which were early ancestors of *Tyrannosaurus rex*.

A lonely *Guanlong* searching for a mate.

One of the skeletons belonged to an adult, and the other was around six years old when it died. The dinosaur was named *Guanlong* and had a large crest on its head. The crest may have been brightly colored. It could have been used to attract a mate.

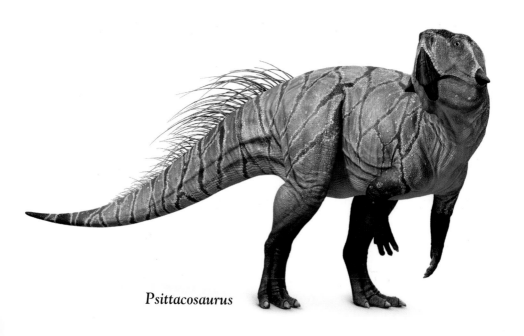

Psittacosaurus

Every dinosaur belongs to a group or family. The dinosaurs in each group have many things in common, even if they don't all look the same. *Psittacosaurus* is one example of this. It belongs to the same group of dinosaurs (ceratopsians) that includes *Triceratops*. However, instead of giant horns, *Psittacosaurus* has quill-like bristles on its back and tail.

The first *Psittacosaurus* remains were collected during an expedition to the Gobi Desert in Mongolia in 1922. Since then, hundreds more have been found. One particular discovery included 30 infants. They were found with an older "babysitter" *Psittacosaurus* who was possibly caring for the youngsters.

Fossil of a *Psittacosaurus* nest with many babies and one adult.

In 1965, Zofia Kielan-Jaworowska and her team found part

Deinocheirus **arm**

of a skeleton in the Gobi Desert. It included huge arms with powerful claws. They named the dinosaur *Deinocheirus*, which means "terrible hand." The missing bones made it difficult for the team to work out what *Deinocheirus* looked like.

It was thought to have been a giant, meat-eating theropod that walked on two legs. For almost 50 years, *Deinocheirus* remained one of the most mysterious dinosaurs ever discovered.

In 2014, the mystery behind the giant claws was solved! Two more skeletons were found. *Deinocheirus* was identified as the largest member of the "ostrichlike" theropod group of dinosaurs.

A *Deinocheirus* walking in a river.

Days of the Dinosaurs

Dinosaurs flourished for more than 165 million years. This time was split into three periods. Follow the lines to match the dinosaurs to when they lived.

Hen with chick

Eoraptor

Styracosaurus

Cetiosaurus

Triassic Period

This period was 252 to 201 million years ago. The first dinosaurs appeared around 231 million years ago.

Jurassic Period

This period was 201 to 145 million years ago. Some of the largest dinosaurs first appeared at this time.

Cretaceous Period

The last of the nonbird dinosaurs died during this period 145 to 66 million years ago.

Today

There are dinosaurs alive today—they are birds!

Living with Dinosaurs

Dinosaurs shared the Earth with many unusual and bizarre creatures. Here are some of the animals that lived alongside them.

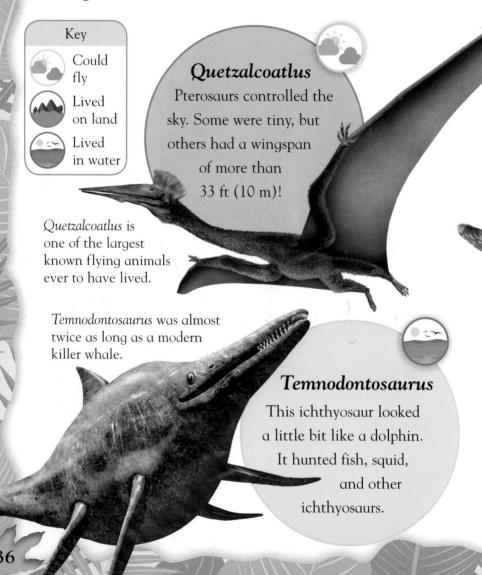

Key

- Could fly
- Lived on land
- Lived in water

Quetzalcoatlus

Pterosaurs controlled the sky. Some were tiny, but others had a wingspan of more than 33 ft (10 m)!

Quetzalcoatlus is one of the largest known flying animals ever to have lived.

Temnodontosaurus was almost twice as long as a modern killer whale.

Temnodontosaurus

This ichthyosaur looked a little bit like a dolphin. It hunted fish, squid, and other ichthyosaurs.

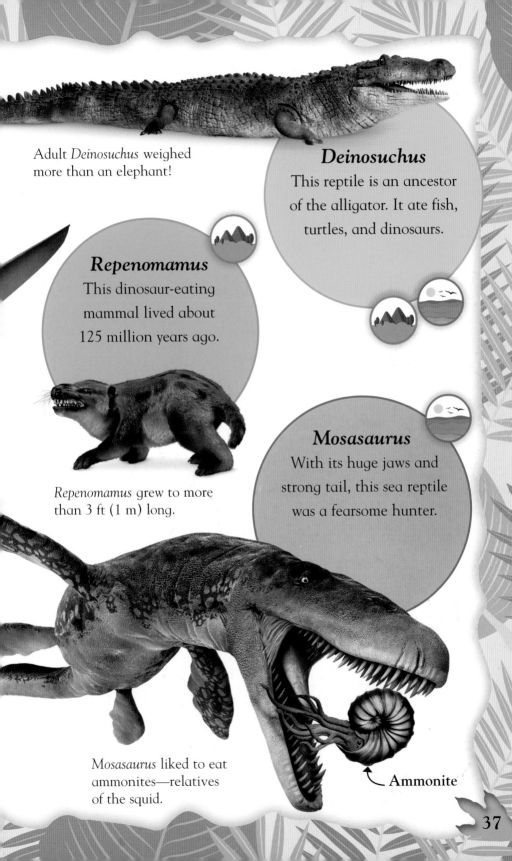

Adult *Deinosuchus* weighed more than an elephant!

Deinosuchus

This reptile is an ancestor of the alligator. It ate fish, turtles, and dinosaurs.

Repenomamus

This dinosaur-eating mammal lived about 125 million years ago.

Repenomamus grew to more than 3 ft (1 m) long.

Mosasaurus

With its huge jaws and strong tail, this sea reptile was a fearsome hunter.

Mosasaurus liked to eat ammonites—relatives of the squid.

Ammonite

Chapter 4

African Adventures

Lots of dinosaur fossils have been collected from all across Africa. In 1976, a cluster of six eggs was found in South Africa. Five eggs contained embryos, or unborn babies. The eggs belonged to a plant-eating dinosaur called *Massospondylus*. They are among the oldest dinosaur embryos in the world.

Another dinosaur that has been found in Africa is *Spinosaurus*. It could live in and out of water and had large spines on its back. The spines formed a sail or hump. This sail may have been used for display or defense, or to help it control its temperature.

An almost complete embryo of *Massospondylus*.

Spinosaurus hunting for food.

There are many large animals alive today, but none that is as tall as the *Giraffatitan* was. It was one of the tallest dinosaurs ever and was twice the height of a giraffe.

One *Giraffatitan* was found in Tanzania. First, paleontologists thought it was a type of *Brachiosaurus*, which lived around 150 million years ago.

After comparing the bones of both dinosaurs, scientists found that they were slightly different. However, the two dinosaurs were both members of the sauropod family.

Sauropod dinosaurs are the heaviest animals to have ever walked on Earth. *Giraffatitan* weighed about the same as five fully grown African elephants!

A wandering herd of *Giraffatitan* feed in a Jurassic forest.

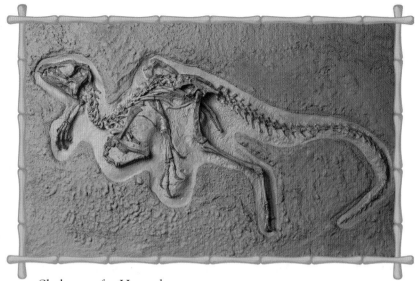

Skeleton of a *Heterodontosaurus*.

In Lesotho, South Africa, between 1961 and 1962, a team of scientists unearthed some grisly remains. They found a skull, a jaw, and some teeth that belonged to an interesting dinosaur.

The dinosaur was called *Heterodontosaurus* and was about the size of a fox. It belonged to a family of dinosaurs called heterodontosaurs. This group had very special teeth. Most dinosaurs had lots of the same type of tooth in their mouths. Heterodontosaurs, however, had many different kinds of teeth. This suggested that they may have been omnivorous, which means that they ate both plants and animals.

Heterodontosaurus may have had coarse bristles on its skin.

Dinosaur Teeth

To work out what a dinosaur ate, look at its teeth. Some herbivores had flat teeth to grind up plants. Carnivores had sharp teeth for tearing flesh.

FACT: Instead of teeth, some dinosaurs, like *Deinocheirus*, had a beak.

This tiny tooth is specially shaped for ripping and grinding up leaves.

These small teeth are sharp and very pointy.

Human molars (the teeth at the back of the mouth) are wide and flat. They are used for grinding.

Stegosaurus

Velociraptor

Human

T. rex teeth were as large as bananas!

Giant sauropods used their teeth to strip leaves off tree branches.

Triceratops had up to 800 teeth just like this one.

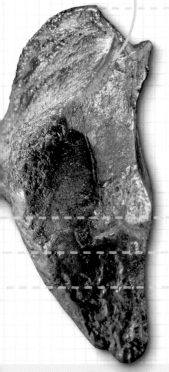

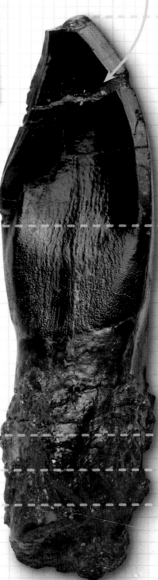

Triceratops

Camarasaurus

Chapter 5

Giants of America

The area that is now North America was once home to some incredible dinosaurs. *Tyrannosaurus*, *Triceratops*, and *Stegosaurus* were just a few that lived there.

The largest dinosaur, *Argentinosaurus*, and the oldest, *Herrerasaurus*, were both found in South America. Many discoveries in America have been very important. They have helped us understand lots about the ancient dinosaur world. Many new finds, such as the berry-eating *Isaberrysaura* from Argentina, continue to be made.

Argentinosaurus had long necks to reach the tops of tall trees.

The dromaeosaurs, often called "raptors," were fast-moving predators. They had sharp teeth and killer claws. Many species were quite small—about the size of a turkey.

In 2005, an incomplete skeleton was found in South Dakota. Ten years later, the bones were studied and identified as a new species. It was called *Dakotaraptor*. It was almost twice as long as a polar bear, making it one of the largest dromaeosaurs known.

Dakotaraptor probably used its feathers to keep warm.

A *Dakotaraptor* claw.

It lived at the same time and in the same area as the giant predator *Tyrannosaurus*.

A series of bumps were found on the arm bones of the skeleton. These are called quill knobs. They suggest that *Dakotaraptor* had feathers.

On Monday, March 21, 2011, news broke that an exciting fossil had been uncovered. It was found at the Millennium Mine in Canada.

Paleontologists Donald Henderson and Darren Tanke visited the site. They inspected the fossil and found, to their amazement, that it was an almost complete armored dinosaur. Named *Borealopelta* in 2017, it is the best-preserved armored dinosaur ever found.

The only specimen of *Borealopelta*.

Skull

It is so well preserved that the 110-million-year-old fossil looks as if it is sleeping. Bits of color were even found in its skin. They show that the animal was reddish brown.

Body armor plates

Spine

Dinosaurs are often found by teams who go looking for them. However, many are found by chance and often in unusual situations.

In 1993, Rubén Carolini was riding a dune buggy in the vast badlands of Patagonia, Argentina. To his surprise, he saw a giant leg bone sticking out of the sand! A team of paleontologists rushed to the scene to see what else they could find.

The species was named *Giganotosaurus carolinii*, in Rubén's honor. The largest skull is just less than 6.5 feet (2 meters) long. *Giganotosaurus* was big enough to rival the famous *Tyrannosaurus rex*. It is the largest carnivorous dinosaur ever found in the southern part of the Earth.

The first skeleton of *Giganotosaurus*, from Argentina.

53

Dinosaurs of Australia and Antarctica

More than 100 million years ago, Australia and Antarctica were joined together. Here are some of the dinosaurs that lived on this ancient land.

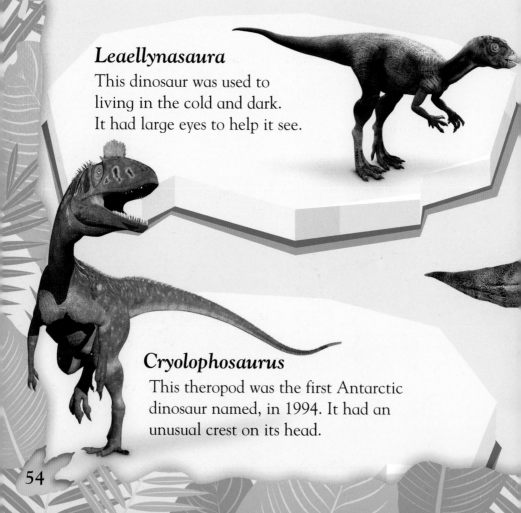

Leaellynasaura
This dinosaur was used to living in the cold and dark. It had large eyes to help it see.

Cryolophosaurus
This theropod was the first Antarctic dinosaur named, in 1994. It had an unusual crest on its head.

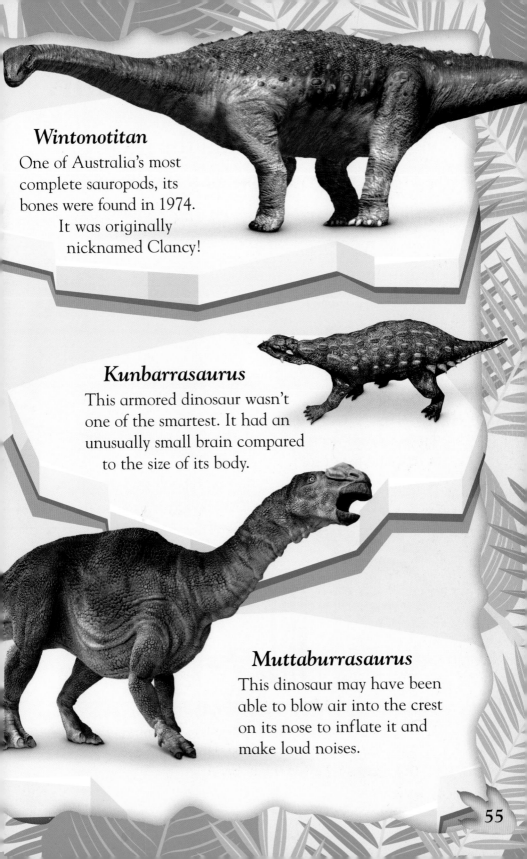

Wintonotitan

One of Australia's most complete sauropods, its bones were found in 1974. It was originally nicknamed Clancy!

Kunbarrasaurus

This armored dinosaur wasn't one of the smartest. It had an unusually small brain compared to the size of its body.

Muttaburrasaurus

This dinosaur may have been able to blow air into the crest on its nose to inflate it and make loud noises.

Can I Find a Dinosaur?

Paleontologists know all the tricks of the trade when it comes to finding fossils. Here are some of them.

Paleontologist's tool kit

Safety glasses
These protect a paleontologist's eyes when they are on a dig.

Notebook and pencil
Paleontologists use these to record their finds.

Brick hammers, chisels, and soft brushes
Some fossils need to be dug up using a hammer and chisel. Brushes help brush dirt off more delicate bones.

The Fossil Collecting Code

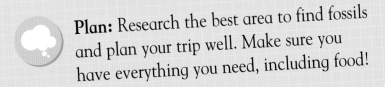

Plan: Research the best area to find fossils and plan your trip well. Make sure you have everything you need, including food!

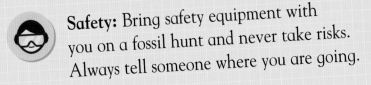

Safety: Bring safety equipment with you on a fossil hunt and never take risks. Always tell someone where you are going.

Patience: Finding fossils can take a little while. Take your time and plan well to get the best results.

Protect: Although fossils have been around for many years, they can be fragile. Look after them so they don't break.

Report: When you have found a fossil, share it with others! Local museums are always interested in new finds.

Quiz

1   What is a paleontologist?

2   Which dinosaur was the first to be named?

3   When did Mary Anning discover the complete plesiosaur skeleton?

4   What did stegosaurs use their tail spikes for?

5   What does *Deinocheirus* mean?

6   Are dinosaurs extinct?

7   Are pterosaurs flying dinosaurs?

8 Which type of dinosaurs were the heaviest?

9 What makes heterodontosaurs unique among dinosaurs?

10 What color was the armored ankylosaur, *Borealopelta*?

11 What is the largest dinosaur on record?

12 Have Australia and Antarctica always been separate?

Answers on page 61

Glossary

Ancestor
Animal or plant to which a more recent animal or plant is related

Badlands
Vast area of land that is often dry, rocky, and difficult to access

Camouflage
Colors or patterns on an animal's skin, fur, or feathers that help it merge with the environment

Carnivore
Meat-eating animal

Ceratopsian
Group of horned dinosaurs that had a frill on their head

Dwarf
Something that is smaller than usual

Embryo
Unborn or unhatched animal

Fossil
Remains or traces of a once-living animal or plant

Herbivore
Plant-eating animal

Paleontologist
Scientist who studies prehistoric life through the examination of fossils

Predator
An animal that lives by hunting and eating other animals

Prehistoric
Ancient time before recorded history

Prey
Animal that is hunted for food

Quill
Stiff, sharp part of a feather or spine

Ravine
Deep, narrow valley

Sand dune
Hill of sand

Sauropod
Group of dinosaurs with long necks and tails

Theropod
Group of meat-eating dinosaurs that stood on two legs

Answers to the quiz:
1. A person who studies dinosaurs and prehistoric life; 2. *Megalosaurus*; 3. 1823; 4. To defend themselves; 5. Terrible hand; 6. They are not extinct; 7. No, they were flying reptiles; 8. Sauropods; 9. Different types of teeth; 10. Reddish brown; 11. *Argentinosaurus*; 12. No, they used to be joined together.

Index

A LEVEL FOR EVERY READER

This book is a part of an exciting four-level reading series to support children in developing the habit of reading widely for both pleasure and information. Each book is designed to develop a child's reading skills, fluency, grammar awareness, and comprehension in order to build confidence and enjoyment when reading.

Ready for a Level 3 (Beginning to Read Alone) Book

A child should:

- Be able to read many words without needing to stop and break them down into sound parts.
- Read smoothly, in phrases and with expression, and at a good pace.
- Self-correct when a word or sentence doesn't sound right or doesn't make sense.

A Valuable and Shared Reading Experience

For many children, reading requires much effort, but adult participation can make reading both fun and easier. Here are a few tips on how to use this book with a young reader:

Check out the contents together:

- Read about the book on the back cover and talk about the contents page to help heighten interest and expectation.
- Ask the reader to make predictions about what he/she thinks will happen next.
- Talk about the information he/she might want to find out.

Encourage fluent reading:

- Encourage reading aloud in fluent, expressive phrases, making full use of punctuation and thinking about the meaning; if helpful, choose a sentence to read aloud to help demonstrate reading with expression.

Praise, share, and talk:

- Notice whether the reader is responding to the text by self-correcting and varying his/her voice.
- Encourage the reader to recall specific details after each chapter.
- Let him/her pick out interesting words and discuss what they mean.
- Talk about what he/she found most interesting or important and show your own enthusiasm for the book.
- Read the quiz at the end of the book and encourage the reader to answer the questions, if necessary, by turning back to the relevant pages to find the answers.

Series consultant, Dr. Linda Gambrell, Emerita Distinguished Professor of Education at Clemson University, has served as President of the National Reading Conference, the College Reading Association and the International Reading Association.